Steel–Oil–Steam

Tuesday Workshop Volunteers, 2019

Steel–Oil–Steam

EVANS+HULF

Acknowledgements and Dedication

Evans+Hulf is a collaboration between Tom Evans and Terry Hulf. The photographs in this book were taken between 2016 and 2020 at the Rolvenden depot of the Kent and East Sussex Railway.

We gratefully acknowledge the help of all the employees, staff and volunteers of the Kent & East Sussex Railway and the 4253 Locomotive company who have helped us in the taking of the photographs and with information for the text. Special thanks are due to David Brenchley (Locomotive Delivery Manager), Andy Hardy (Service Delivery Manager) and all those whose portraits are seen here. We apologise to all of those whose words or images we have not been able to include for reasons of space.

The book is dedicated to the memory of the late Rodney Grey de Charmoy, who gave the 1886 Chapman 'British' camera to Tom Evans.

Foreword

It was almost 60 years ago that I first came to know the Kent & East Sussex Railway. In those days Rolvenden yard seemed a scene of desolation, of folk memory and, one might fancy, of ghosts. Above the grass-grown track only the platform mound and the water tower loomed as reminders of what had been. Six hectic decades later Rolvenden is again the site of a busy locomotive yard and works. Both of these perceptions may stand as a metaphor for the heritage era of this historic and much-loved light railway. The achievements which may now be seen are mirrored along the entire length of the line from Tenterden to Bodiam and may yet extend further to Robertsbridge.

This book is focused on Rolvenden, and rightly so for, whilst all aspects of railway history deserve equal respect, it is the steam locomotive which is at the core of that heritage. Rolvenden is where the K&ESR's steam locomotives receive skilled care and in the light of early morning are brought into life as the railway's beating heart. A railway is of course not just machines it is a community of people and it is entirely appropriate that Steel-Oil-Steam includes people as much as it does locomotives thereby bringing depth and humanity to the subject.

Tom Evans and Terry Hulf's use of a vintage camera and atmospheric monochrome provides a rounded unity in presenting Rolvenden Works and the Kent & East Sussex Railway. In this enticing volume, traditional techniques have been used to create a work which will be produced using modern technology. That is what heritage railways are all about; making what has been live again and have a place in what is and what will be.

Nick Pallant, summer 2020

Nick Pallant writes on the history of the Kent & East Sussex Railway in the heritage era. He has worked on the K&ESR both as a volunteer and an employee. He was Company Secretary from 2001 to 2016 and continues to edit the Tenterden Terrier house journal at the time of writing.

Steel–Oil–Steam

At half-past six on a fine summer morning, Rolvenden station looks deserted. The crossing gates are closed, the signals all at stop and the rails gleam in the low sun. The platform is dressed like a stage set, with ancient luggage and enamel signs. A new poster shows a Spitfire in the sky, artfully foregrounded against the steam and smoke rising from a tank engine pulling a little train of three green coaches through lush countryside with the caption *HISTORY: Travel through time with the K&ESR*.

On the swelling curve of the meadow, sheep and their fattening lambs graze peacefully, their contented 'baas' drifting across the yard, and a thrush sings loudly in the trees beside the line. Everything is very peaceful in the Kent countryside.

Behind the scenes, it takes hard, skilled work to maintain the nostalgic illusions of a heritage railway.

In the sidings between the platform and the hillside, two engines are being prepared to run the day's trains. There is a pleasant smell of wood smoke as the fires are lit with kindling and oil-soaked rags, but as coal is added, the smell changes. Acrid sulphur fumes fill the air, catch in the throat and leave a sour taste in the mouth. Black smoke rises from the engines' chimneys to be replaced by a haze of hot, clear gases as the fires build to a cleaner burn.

The first people to arrive in the yard are the steam-raiser's and the cleaners. They open up, turn off the alarms, read the notice board and make tea before starting work. It is the steam raiser's responsibility to make sure that each engine has its wheels chocked and carries a 'not to be moved' safety notice. He—or she—checks the water levels in the rostered locomotives to make sure there are no leaks and only then, when certain that everything is safe, do they light the fires.

Visitor expectations are high. Every morning, the working engines are cleaned and polished until they gleam, leaving none of the dirt they would have carried in the days when all railways ran on steam. The cleaners wear nitrile gloves to protect their hands from the kerosene they use to remove the grime and ash from the wheels, frames and motion. Once the muck is off, they wash and wax the paintwork until it gleams. Some cleaners like to give the matt-finished smokeboxes a coat of oil to make them shine, but oil collects grime, which will have to be cleaned and scrubbed off the next day.

Firemen and drivers arrive an hour after the steam raiser. While the fireman checks the gauges, cleans the cab and collects the safety gear and lamps from the stores, the driver fills the reservoirs that lubricate the locomotive's moving parts. Oil cups to the crank pin and crosshead bearings are closed with simple corks, with a porous cane to let in air—a solution that dates from the early days of steam and still works better than a modern grease point. Oil reservoirs that lubricate the cylinders are topped up with another oil, formulated to vaporise in the steam and form a protective film for the cylinders and pistons.

Cleaners, steam-raisers, firemen and engine-drivers are all volunteers, men and women alike. In many cases, the fascination with steam goes back to early childhood and family traditions. Volunteering can start in schooldays and continue well into retirement. A fireman must be at least eighteen years old and a driver twenty-one but there is no upper age limit, although the medicals become increasingly stringent with age. Volunteering may begin from a romantic attachment to the idea of steam but it matures into a deeper engagement with the engineering and technology, which is sufficient to endure the discomforts that midwinter weather can bring to outdoor work.

Volunteers start as locomotive cleaners. After a year or eighteen months, they may train to become steam-raisers and firemen. After two years as a fireman, a volunteer may begin to train as a driver. Members of the railway staff provide cover and supervise training, recording the trainee's progress in a logbook. On completing the logbook, the trainee driver must take practical and theory tests to become a 'passed fireman' or probationary driver. Full qualification is subject to completing a round trip to the satisfaction of a very experienced Inspector.

So strong is the passion for steam is that many volunteers spend their holidays working on a different line. Heidi Mowforth drives on the K&ESR as a holiday break from driving on the Bluebell Line; Beth Furness comes to Kent from York, where she works for the National Railway Museum but drives as a volunteer on the North Yorkshire line. When steam is raised, the locomotive makes a contented bubbling and boiling sound; the driver tests the brakes and fills the sanders, which help stop the wheels slipping on the steep incline up to Tenterden Town station.

A telescopic handler—a machine like a tractor, with a large bucket on a hydraulic arm—drives up and fills the engine's bunker with coal. Ordinary coal contains a mixture of carbon, ash, sulphur, nitrogen, oxygen, and hydrogen. Sulphur is bad news both for the environment and the locomotive, eating away at the boiler. It is sulphur that causes brown smoke from the chimney and acid in the air. Dark smoke may look dramatic but a good fire should burn with almost clear exhaust. It is the fireman's job to optimise performance and efficiency by adding and distributing coal, controlling the air supply and using the blower to pull exhaust gases up the chimney.

Each locomotive uses about a boiler-full of water on the round trip from Tenterden to Bodiam and back. Untreated mains water contains many impurities, which are deposited as limescale on the boiler tubes and walls when it boils. Limescale's insulating properties cause the inner surfaces of the tubes to grow very hot, seriously reducing the engine's efficiency. On time, excessive heat will corrode the metal; if allowed to develop unchecked, limescale will eventually cause a boiler to fail.

British Rail hardly bothered about water quality but the K&ESR takes pride in meticulous water treatment. Water chemist Liam Head has installed a reverse osmosis plant to removes heavy metals, minerals and electrolytes and produce purified water. Pure water, though, is a super solvent, which would strip chemicals from the locomotives' boilers, so a carefully calculated amount of 'raw' water is added back. The resulting treated water will clean the tubes and stop any build-up of limescale without attacking the boiler. Every three trips, the locomotive's water tank is dosed with tannin, which turns the stripped limescale to mud. Sludge and debris that has collected in the boiler is cleared in a 'blowdown' when the driver opens a valve and all the muck is blasted out in a cloud of steam.

Finally, the first locomotive is ready for the day's work and puffs off up the line to Tenterden Town Station where it will join the carriages for the first train of the day.

A smell of sulphur lingers in the air, fumes catching in the throat and prickling the eyes, but the staff and volunteers no longer notice. The sounds of locomotives are replaced by the percussive noise of hammering and riveting, the buzz of grinding and the crackle of welding from beyond the open doors of the workshop.

Steam engines need constant maintenance. Even with the best treatment, water quality deteriorates in the boiler, residue accumulates and this may produce large bubbles that carry water into the steam delivery system. Unlike steam, water is not compressible: if trapped in the cylinder, there is a risk of fracture and failure to the cylinder head and piston. Every twenty-eight days the boiler is given a washout, drained and cleaned to remove the accumulated residue.

A boiler surveyor inspects the locomotive once a year; after ten years, the boiler certificate expires, the engine is taken out of service and the boiler is completely rebuilt. At the same time, every part of the engine is stripped down, refurbished and re-assembled in an overhaul that takes at least four or five years, depending on the scale of necessary repairs, the availability of money and skilled labour.

The unexpected is normal and frequently expensive. World War Two tank engines, built in the States for the US army in Europe, had a design life of only five years. More than seventy years later, *Wainwright* (masquerading as its sister engine *Frank S. Ross*) is still steaming up and down the Rother Valley while *Maunsell*, K&ESR's other 'Yank tank,' is in the workshops for an overhaul. When *Maunsell* was stripped, the fitters found that a major structural component—a heavy steel stretcher connecting the main frames—had come to the end of its life and needed to be replaced.

In an age when skills are increasingly specialised and metalwork is divided between different specialist firms, a heritage locomotive workshop is one of the very few places where a fitter can expect to do everything from blacksmithing to fabrication, from heavy engineering to fine precision machining and making safety critical parts. K&ESR can carry out most tasks in its Rolvenden works, short of casting steel, making a complete boiler, or turning wheels and fitting steel tyres.

Almost any part of a hundred-year-old locomotive may fail at any time. Joints in steam and water tubes spring leaks; gauges break; bolts shear; wheels wear out, and so on. In 2019, the axle bearings on the pannier tank engine 1638 ran so hot that the white metal liners melted. Accidents in the locomotive's past had distorted its frames, causing friction in the axle boxes. In the workshop, the engine was lifted and propped on blocks, the wheels were lowered and the axle boxes removed. Remnants of white metal were melted out, new liners were cast, machined and fitted to the axle with a little extra clearance to allow the engine to run sweetly and avoid overheating.

Though few in number, the engineering staff have a wide range of skills and experience. Workshop supervisor Adrian Landi started out as an electrical engineer. After being made redundant, he applied for a job as a locomotive fitter, thinking he would give it a try for a year or two. Quarter of a century later he is still there, having progressed from general metalworking and fabrication to boilersmithing and a supervisory role.

Volunteering is a more usual route to a paid job on the railway. Dan Dickson worked for a heavy engineering company while volunteering first as a fireman and then as a driver. Now he is employed full-time as a locomotive fitter and trainee boilersmith, but still continues to drive as a volunteer. Liam Head studied geology at university before working on large-scale lake management. Volunteering led to a job as a fitter, machinist and water scientist, setting up and managing the water treatment plant of which the railway is so proud. Young Jamie Clapp visited the K&ESR with his Nan as a fourteen-year-old, asking "how do I start as a volunteer?" The next day he went out on an engine. After leaving school, went to work for the railway as an apprentice; now he spends four days a week at Rolvenden and one studying at college. Every day in the workshop and yard is different, working under supervision on anything and everything—making new bolts for engines, washing out cylinders, changing springs, turning new bushes on the lathe, painting and cleaning. After his apprenticeship, Jamie hopes to get a job here as a fitter's mate until he is twenty-one and then go to work on the main-line railway, which offers better pay and more scope for a career.

Most of the locomotive department staff are qualified shunters so that whoever is on duty can move rolling stock at any time. Engines also have to be tested in steam after repair, before going back into service. Three of the shed staff are qualified drivers and the apprentice Jamie is being fast-tracked to train as a fireman.

Volunteers come from every kind of occupation and background—school students, professional railwaymen and women, engineers, bankers, computer and IT professionals, teachers, policemen, postmen, a press photographer, a vicar and so on. They are not only cleaners, firemen and drivers: there is a floating army of workshop and yard volunteers who do everything from painting to metalwork, machining, blacksmithing, riveting and welding.

On Tuesdays and Sundays, a swarm of volunteer workers descends on the workshop, the yard and the shed where they are reconstructing a once-derelict locomotive. 4253 is a 2-8-0 heavy tank engine, built for the Great Western Railway in 1917 to haul long coal trains through the Welsh valleys. In 1963 it was sold to the scrap yard in Barry and then, in 1987 to the Pontypool and Blaenavon Railway, where it continued to sit out in the open, unrestored. A company was formed to buy 4253 for service on the K&ESR: in 2011 the engine was moved to Rolvenden and restoration began. After half a century exposed to the elements, some of the components were only usable as patterns and many other parts were missing. Nine years later, the locomotive is beginning to take shape again. Once a fortnight, the project's chief engineer Henry Mowforth, who works as a boilersmith for the Bluebell Line, returns to Rolvenden to check the work, train volunteers and solve problems.

In the evening, the workshops are closed and the locomotives return to the yard after their final run. The water tanks are filled, the driver stops the engine over the pit and makes it safe. The fireman opens the smokebox door and shovels out the ash into a wheelbarrow, drops the fire, hoses down the embers and rakes out the ash from the firebox into the pit. The driver turns off all the auxiliary systems, rolls the locomotive into its place for the night and puts on the chimney cap to keep in the heat. Ready for the night, the locomotive gently simmers down and the yard falls quiet.

Rolvenden Yard from the Trackside, 2020

"A steam engine is the most spectacular and engaging form of power. You can see it, hear it and smell it. The exhaust steam, smoke, and motion stimulate all the senses"

Richard Moffatt

"Lighting locomotives on a fine summer morning is peaceful and very pleasant."

Chris Davey

"I particularly like the science of steam. The three laws of thermodynamics developed form studying the questions raised by the first steam engines and the need to know what to boil and how to heat it to make the best use of the available energy."

Liam Head

Norwegian Blowing Down, 2019

Rolvenden Yard and Trackside, 2019

Workshop Doors, 2016

Rolvenden Yard With 0–6–0 Pannier Tank 1638, 2016

Rolvenden Yard With *Norwegian* and *Northiam* Getting Up Steam, 2019

'Yank Tank' *Frank S. Ross,* 2019

Shovels and Brooms, 2018

Steel Wool, 2019

Cleaners' Store, 2018

From the Workshop to the Yard, 2018

"I've been crazy about steam trains since I was a little girl."

Courtenay Jane Forder

"I was introduced to steam railways very early in life by my granddad.
If I had known it was possible to be paid to work on one, I would have joined
as an apprentice instead of going to university."

Liam Head

"Steam railways are a consuming passion, different from everyday life,
in the company of good people."

Angus Entwhistle

Heidi Mowforth, Volunteer Driver, 2019

Chris Davey, Volunteer Steam Raiser and Fireman, 2018

Courtenay Jane Forder, Volunteer Cleaner, 2019

Sheila McKenna, Volunteer Steam Raiser, 2019

Angus Entwhistle, Volunteer Fireman, 2018

Beth Furness, Volunteer Driver, 2019

Courtenay Jane Forder Cleaning 25 *Northiam*, 2019

Early Morning in the Yard, 1638 and *Norwegian*, 2019

Shovels and Irons, 2019

Outside the Shed, 2018

"We still have to build roads, railways and physical infrastructure, we have to make things. All the work here is hands on, you can see what you are doing and achieve a physical result, unlike a computer game where there is nothing tangible."

Henry Mowforth

"It is fascinating to see a locomotive being reduced to its component parts— and then to see it grow back into a gleaming, painted engine in steam again."

David Brenchley

Driving Wheel of 32678 *Knowle* Under Overhaul, 2019

Steam Crane in Operation, 2019

Steam Crane, 2019

David Dee Steam-Cleaning the Pit, 2018

Workshop Interior, Boilers and Welding Gear, 2019

Charwelton Undergoing Major Overhaul, 2018

Charwelton in the Workshop, 2018

"It's real life here. Everyone has come to do something they really want to do, maintaining working machines."

Richard Moffat

"Metal is like a living substance: it moves and shifts. There are things about metal you can't teach but have to learn through experience. A man who knows what he is doing can hit a piece of distorted metal or heat it, jut so, with the right force in exactly the right spot and it will be straight and true. Missing the spot by just half-an-inch would make it worse."

Adrian Landi

"You need a feel for steel: you use all your senses and you get to know by feel when some-thing is right. It's hard to explain but you can tell at once if someone has got it."

Dan Dickson

"I wake up in the morning looking forward to going to work and hate it at the end of the day when I have to go home. I would love to just stay and carry on."

Jamie Clapp

Richard Moffatt, Fitter, Volunteer and Director of 4253 Locomotive Ltd, 2019

Jamie Clapp, Apprentice Fitter and Trainee Fireman, 2019

Liam Head, Water Chemist and Fitter, 2019

Dan Dickson, Fitter and Trainee Boilersmith, 2018

David Dee, Yard Assistant and Locomotive Department Administrator, 2019

Jamie Clapp Working on the Diesel Shunter, 2019

Tools by the Inspection Pit, 2019

Welding Gear, 2018

Protective Headgear, 2019

White Metal Kit, 2018

Welding Gear Cables, 2019

"The locomotives are very old and there are no instruction manuals. Every job is a challenge. Often we have to work out a way to do the job and then to make the tools to do it."

Jerry Preston-Ladd

"When I began working on 4253, I had no engineering skills. I didn't even know how to use a grinder. Now, I can carry out hot riveting and work on the copper firebox without supervision."

Dave Dee

"Once you start, it just gets you. The best bit is the camaraderie. It's like working in industry in the old days: you just get on with it, taking responsibility. We've done so many projects that we can turn our hands to almost anything now."

Charlie Masterson

John Arlet, Volunteer, 2018

Charlie Masterson, Volunteer Driver and Director 4253 locomotive Ltd, 2019

Boiler and Extractor Tubes, 2019

Welding and Grinding Bay, 2018

Norman Thompson, Volunteer, 2018

Richard Stone, Volunteer, 2018

Forge Tools, 2019

Shackles and Chains, 2019

Adrian Landi, Worshop Supervisor, 2019

Steve Armstrong, Volunteer, 2019

Jerry Preston-Ladd, Volunteer and Director of 4253 Locomotive Ltd, 2020

Spanners, Washout Plugs and Fusible Plugs, 2019

Protective Gear, 2020

Radial Drill, 2018

Milling Machine, Chuck and Oilcan, 2018

Workshop Tool Cupboard, 2018

Warning and Status Boards, 2018

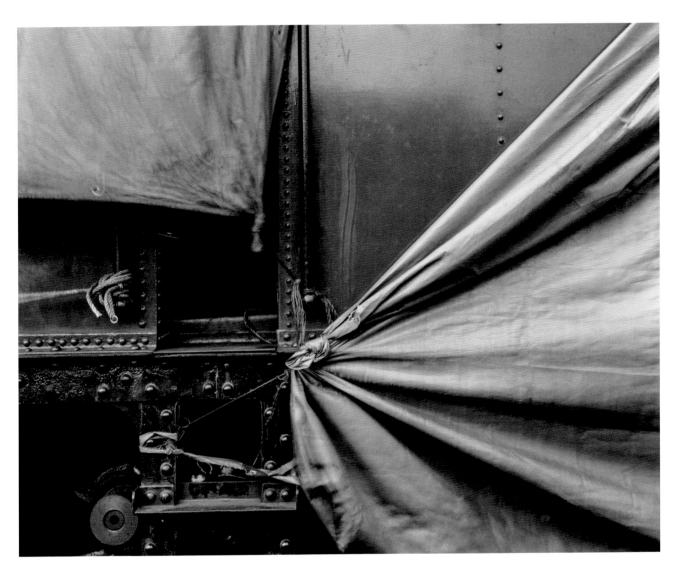

4253 Under Tarpaulin, 2019

1638 Protected against the Frost, 2019

Henry Mowforth, Boilersmith, Volunteer, and Director 4253 locomotive Ltd, 2019

4253 Boiler, 2019

Norwegian and Centenary Crew, 2019

Emptying the Smokebox of 25 *Northiam*, 2019

Norwegian Air Pump Under Wraps, 2019

Rolvenden, Looking Down the Line, 2019

The Chapman 'British' Camera

Evans+Hulf work with a 15 x 12" ultra-large-format camera made by J. T. Chapman in Manchester in the 1880s. Josiah Chapman (1843-1907) was a chemist who, in the 1870s, developed improved formulae for producing dry gelatin-bromide plates. A shrewd businessman, he then designed and sold cameras to use his plates, starting with the quarter-plate 'Manchester' camera in 1883 followed by the 'British' range in 1886. 15 x 12" was the largest model.

This camera originally belonged to James Mudd, a pioneer of industrial photography, who with his assistant and successor George Grundy used it to photograph the railway engines built at the Beyer Peacock works in Manchester. The original ground-glass screen has a series of pencilled guides marked 'engine' and 'engine and tender'.

Our camera has survived with its original lens and three double dark slides. Restoration has been kept to the minimum needed to make the camera light-proof and all the interventions are reversible. The lens is a Dallmeyer Rapid Rectilinear, serial number 24042, recorded in the Dallmeyer stock book on 27 May 1875. It has a focal length of 19.5" (about 500mm) and a very fine iris diaphragm with f-stops from f8 for f32. A bulb-operated Packard shutter, of a type invented toward the end of the nineteenth century, has been mounted in front of the lens. The double-sided 'book slide' plate-holders open with a hinge and were designed to take two glass plates, back to back, separated by a metal spacer with springs that keep the plates firmly seated.

Exposures are made on Agfa X-ray film, held in place by aluminium sheet spacers. The film is orthochromatic, as opposed to panchromatic, sensitive to green light, but (like nineteenth-century emulsions) not to red. The outfit is heavy, and it takes two people to operate the cumbersome and fragile camera safely. Setting up, focusing the image, fitting the dark slide and making an exposure takes significant time. Snapshots and action photography are impossible; exposures are long and the depth of field shallow. Every image is the result of careful joint decisions about subject, viewpoint, framing and exposure.

Processed negatives are scanned to make high-resolution uncompressed 16-bit black-and-white digital master files, which are digitally corrected and spotted before printing or exporting for reproduction or the Web publication.

Steel–Oil–Steam

All photographs © Tom Evans and Terry Hulf, Evans+Hulf, evans-hulf.com
Foreword © Nick Pallant
Text © Tom Evans

Rear cover photograph: 1638 Raising Steam, 2018

First edition 2020

Published by Samson Press

ISBN 978-0-95-309511-7

British Library Cataloguing in Publications Data
A catalogue record of this book is available from the British Library

Cover design by Karen Wilks
Printed in England by Pureprint, Uckfield